W9-CNW-124

GIRLS' GUIDES

Best Buds

A Girl's Guide to Friendship

Victoria Shaw

the rosen publishing group's
rosen central
new york

Published in 2000 by The Rosen Publishing Group, Inc.
29 East 21st Street, New York, NY 10010

First Edition

Library of Congress Cataloging-in-Publication Data

Shaw, Victoria.
    Best buds : a girl's guide to friendship / by Victoria Shaw. —
1st ed.
        p.   cm. — (Girls guides)
    Summary: Describes the importance of friendships among preteen and teenage girls, offering advice on choosing and getting along with friends.
    ISBN 0-8239-2987-6
    1. Teenage girls—United States—Attitudes Juvenile literature.
    2. Teenage girls—United States—Psychology Juvenile literature.
    3. Female friendships—United States Juvenile literature.
    4. Interpersonal relations—United States Juvenile literature
    5. Peer pressure in adolescence—United States Juvenile literature.
    [1. Teenage girls.   2. Friendship.   3. Interpersonal relations.]
    I. Title.   II. Series.
HQ798.S464   1999
305.235   dc21   99-15071
                                                                        CIP

Manufactured in the United States of America

Contents

About This Book

The middle school years are like a roller coaster—wild and scary but also fun and way cool. One minute you're way, way up there, and the next minute you're plunging down into the depths. Not surprisingly, sometimes you may find yourself feeling confused and lost. Not to worry, though. Just like on a roller-coaster ride, at the end of all this crazy middle school stuff, you'll be laughing and screaming and talking about how awesome it all was.

Right now, however, chances are your body is changing so much that it's barely recognizable, your old friends may not share your interests anymore, and your life at school is suddenly hugely complicated. And let's not even get into the whole boy issue. It's a wonder that you can still think straight at all.

Fortunately, reader dear, help is here. This book is your road map. It's also a treasure chest filled with ideas and advice. Armed with this book and with your own inner strength (trust us, you have plenty), you can safely, confidently navigate the twists and turns of your middle school years. It will be tough going, and sometimes you'll wonder if you'll ever get through it. But you—fabulous, powerful, unique you—are up to the task. This book is just a place to start.

A friend is someone you can call when you ace your math test or get a valentine from your crush. You can tell her your deepest secrets—and know that they'll stay secrets. A good friend is there for you when you need her. She knows what to say to make you laugh hysterically even when you feel as if you're going to cry. And although she sometimes drives you nuts, you know you'll get over it because she's your friend.

Everybody needs friends, but in the teen and preteen years, you really need them. By the time you hit your teens, you'll probably find that tagging along with your parents just doesn't cut it anymore. You want to test your wings and start feeling more independent. You want to hang with people your own age who share your interests and can understand what you're going through. Your buds help you feel safe and secure as you make your way toward adulthood.

Changing Friendships

When you were younger, you probably didn't care much about who your friends were. You just hung out with the kids around you, like your next-door neighbor or the girl who sat next to you in class. But as you grow older, you may find that your friends are more about choice than convenience. Rather than just spending time with the gal next door, teens and preteens are more likely to choose friends with similar interests and values. That often means that you will find yourself drifting away from old friends.

The good news about your changing friendships is that you'll probably start to have much more in common with your buds. The friends you have now are more likely to marvel over your photo collection of Leo or help you to train to be the next Sheryl Swoopes. The bad news is that as the old gang grows apart, you may feel sad about losing the security and familiarity of the friendships you once had. And if your old friends pull away before you do, you may feel kind of left out. Relax. Part of growing up is figuring out where you fit in. It may take some time, but you'll find friends who are right for you.

Got Questions? Get Answers!

This book will answer your questions about friendship: How to make new friends. What it takes to be a good friend. And how to deal when you and your buds don't see eye-to-eye on important issues. You'll learn the truth about popularity and why peer pressure isn't always the worst thing in the world. But this book is just the beginning. In the sections at the end, you'll find even more books, Web sites, and other resources for exploring the wonderful world of friendship.

This book focuses on girls' friendships with girls. Girls and guys can be friends too, of course, and some of the same rules that apply to gal pals also work for guy pals. There are also some big differences, but in the end, a friend is a friend.

How to Be a Good Friend

2

Dear Vicky,
I told my best bud that I was crushing over this guy in chem class. I thought the news was strictly between us, but she blabbed it to the whole school. Now I'm totally embarrassed because everyone, including my crush, knows my secret. What should I do?
—Crushed

Dear Crushed,
Sounds as though you may need to find yourself a new best friend. Revealing secrets is a definite friendship DON'T (no matter how juicy the scoop)! Maybe your pal hasn't learned the rules yet, so you could give her a second chance. But keep your secrets to yourself for a while—just in case.

What makes a person a good friend? A good friend is someone you enjoy being with, who has similar interests, and who values your friendship as much as you value hers. You know that you can trust her and that she can put her trust in you.

Do you have what it takes to be a good friend? Take the following quiz to figure out your GFQ (your Good Friend Quotient, that is).

Ms. Quiz: Are You a Good Friend?

1. You're coming to the end of what was definitely the worst day of your life. You got dogged on your English test, you missed all of your shots in b-ball practice, and your parents refused to give you that much-needed advance on your allowance. You're all set to start screaming into your pillow when your bud calls to share some mega-great news. How do you react?

(a) You listen patiently to her news and try to be as enthusiastic as you can.

(b) You cut her off mid-sentence and start in on the details of your horrible day. After all, given the circumstances, she couldn't possibly expect you to be happy for her.

2. Your bud confesses that she is totally sweating this guy in your math class, who you've heard is really bad news. When she asks your opinion, you:

(a) Tell her to proceed with caution—you've heard some not-so-great things about her crush. Then you remind her that since rumors can be wrong, she should trust her own instincts.

(b) Tell her, in no uncertain terms, that her guy is a loser. Then go on and on about how she's once again shown the worst possible judgment in the choosing-a-crush department.

3. Your pal just told you what could turn out to be the juiciest piece of gossip you've heard all year. The only problem is that she's the subject. What do you do?

(a) Hear her out, give her a hug, and reassure her that you'll take her secret with you to the grave.

(b) Carefully take note of every detail, since you plan to spread the news ASAP. After all, your friend couldn't possibly expect you to keep info this newsworthy to yourself.

4. Your friend tells you about her burning desire to join the chess club. Personally, you think that the chess club is a one-way ticket to Geeksville. When she asks you if you want to join too, you:

(a) Tell her that chess just isn't your game, but she that should go ahead and join if she wants to. You're glad that she's found something that really interests her.

(b) Burst out laughing! You tell her that you wouldn't be caught dead with those geeks. And ditto for her if she even thinks of joining the club.

Answers:
Wondering if you passed the test? Here's a clue: If you picked mostly As, congratulations! It sounds as if you're trustworthy and thoughtful—you've got what it takes to be a good friend. But if your answers were mostly Bs, you may need some tutoring in the subject of friendship. To see where you went right or wrong, let's take a closer look at each of the answers.

1. A good friend tries to be a *good listener*, even when she's got other things on her mind. Don't rain on your pal's parade just because you had a less-than-perfect day. Who knows? Maybe some of her cheeriness will rub off on you.

2. A good friend is someone whom you can *trust*. Good friends never reveal secrets or talk behind each other's backs . . . period!

3. A good friend knows how to be *honest and supportive without judging too much*. When a pal shows a lapse in judgment, a good friend is always honest, but not to the point of making her bud feel bad about herself.

4. Good friends *accept each other for who they are*. If your bud likes to hang out with brains, more power to her. The fact that she can play a good game of chess and still blab for hours about her favorite soap star is what makes her so special.

Getting back to our original question: What makes a good friend? In a nutshell, a good friend is someone who can be trusted and knows how to compromise. You like to do a lot of the same stuff and talk about the same things. She's a good listener who can be honest without being overly judgmental. Finally, a good friend values your friendship just as you value hers, and she accepts you for who you are.

Making Friends

3

Whether you're the new girl in school, one of many girls in a new school, or just an old girl looking for a new crew, making friends can be challenging—especially if you have to make the first move. After all, maybe that girl in your English class seems like gal pal material, but how do you break the ice? And what if she doesn't have an equally high opinion of you? It's almost as hard as talking to your crush for the first time, and in a way, the same types of feelings are at stake. When you reach out to someone new, you put yourself on the line, and that can be scary. But trust me, finding a good friend is worth the risk.

Finding Ms. Right

Who's your perfect pal? If you're looking for someone who shares your passion for chemistry, a fellow scientist may be your ideal bud. If you are aching to go to the right parties and to hang with the "in" crowd, then choosing friends who are popular may be high on your list. But remember, when it comes to friends, some qualities are more important than others. Sure, the girl might be popular and pretty and wear trendy clothes, but if she can't keep a secret or be kind to her pals, what's the point?

There's no way to tell if someone will make a good friend just by looking at her. It will take some time before you know whether or not you're going to click. Still, if you find a person who seems likeable and enjoys some of the same stuff that you do, you're off to a good

start. If you're feeling superlonely, you may be tempted to join the "wrong" crowd. You know who I mean: the kids who are always getting into trouble or who treat each other in a not-so-friendly way. The fact is that no matter how bad you feel, you won't be the least bit better off with pals who are unkind, who pressure you to do dumb things, or who lack basic values of right and wrong.

So how do you find the right group of pals? There are

dozens of ways. Ask that girl who sits behind you in math what she thought about yesterday's homework. Try signing up for an after-school club or doing some volunteer work. The trick is to find something that interests you and get involved. After all, it's really easy to strike up a conversation over a soccer game or after a dance class because you'll already have something to talk about. Another big plus about getting involved is that you'll be too busy to feel lonely.

Breaking the Ice

Now that you've found someone you'd like to get to know better, the next step is . . . getting to know her better. Before you approach a prospective pal, you may want to test the waters first. If you catch her eye in class, does she smile back or look the other way? If she acts friendly, chances are she's looking for a friend. But you should also keep in mind that some gals may seem as though they're blowing you off when they're really just shy. So if she seems like the wallflower type, you may want to give her more than one chance.

Sometimes all you have to do is smile and say "hi." From there, you can chat about stuff you have in common, like the super-tough math test you just suffered through ("Was that test a killer, or what?") or the fact that you're wearing the same shoes ("Where'd you buy yours?"). Everyone loves a compliment, so if you dig her sweater, don't be too shy to ask where she bought it. But don't spread it on too thick, or it may seem as if you're trying too hard.

If you're thinking to yourself, "I could never walk up to a stranger and start talking," I hear ya. Making new friends can be scary, especially if you're shy to begin with. And I'm not going to tell you that making the first move isn't a huge risk. You might end up feeling embarrassed or rejected. But you also might make a great friend to last a lifetime.

Dealing with Rejection

I'd like to be able to give you my word that everyone you meet will think you're the coolest chick ever. Unfortunately, unless you're magically charmed, making new friends means risking rejection. If the worst does happen, and the person

you approach totally blows you off, try not to take it too personally. I know that sounds like the hugest line ever, but the honest truth is that it's her loss. If the person is rude or supercold, you can consider yourself lucky. Nobody needs friends like that, anyway.

Finding new friends may take a while. You might feel as though you're getting more than your share of rejection, but hang in there. It's worth it!

Cliques: In, Out, or Undecided

Good or bad, cliques are a fact of school life. By the time they make it to junior high, lots of people already have found a group of pals, large or small, to hang with. Being in a clique can give you a ready-made support group. You'll have people around who support and care about you. Plus you'll never have to worry about being friendless on Saturday night.

Members of a clique usually have similar interests, backgrounds, and values. That's part of the reason why cliques have different nicknames and reputations (e.g., jocks, techno-geeks, stoners). Being like the rest of your group can be great up to a point—if that's truly who you are. But some cliques take the conformity thing too far. When you join a clique, you shouldn't have to leave your individuality at the door. If your pals try to control things such as the clothes you wear, the people you talk to, or the guys you date, it may be time to find a new group of friends.

Ms. Quiz: Is Your Clique Right for You?

Finding the right crew can be great. But not all cliques are created equal. Before you try to join a new clique (or decide whether or not to stick with the clique you're in), ask yourself if any of the following statements are true:

1. The members of the clique don't really share your interests.
2. Your pals have a reputation for raising hell and getting themselves into serious trouble.
3. Your buds would go crazy if you even thought about hanging out with or, even worse, dating someone who wasn't in the clique.
4. Your pals try to pressure you to do things that are against your better judgment.
5. The clique is superselective and can be extremely snotty when it comes to outsiders.
6. When the clique is down on someone, for whatever reason, they just freeze that person out with no explanation or say rude things about the person behind his or her back.
7. When you're with your pals, you don't feel like yourself, and you feel a ton of pressure to act like your buds so you'll fit in.
8. Being in the clique is not as much fun as you thought it would be.

If you answered "true" to any of the statements, you may want to reconsider your choice of friends. Members of a clique—or any group of friends—should be kind to one another. They should enjoy doing some of the same things without limiting each other's interests and activities. Finally, members of a clique should respect each other as individuals.

Are You Clique Material?

Not everyone's a joiner. Maybe being in a clique puts too much pressure on you to act a certain way. Or you're having trouble finding a crowd that matches your interests. Some people are happiest with just one or two close friends. Others are more comfortable having friends in a few different cliques rather than spending all their time with just one group. The most important thing is finding people whom you enjoy and on whom you can depend. The rest will fall into place.

Being cliqueless can also have a downside, though. If you have friends in several different cliques, you may feel left out when your buds are involved in activities that are limited to their clique. And you may miss out on some of the socializing that goes along with being in a group. If you don't have a ton of casual friends, you may not get invited to every party or be up on all of the latest gossip. But you probably will have more time to spend with the one or two people you really care about. It's up to you to decide what matters most to you.

When Your Folks Hate Your Friends

So you've found the perfect clique, but there's one small problem: Your parents are less than thrilled with your selection. The first question to ask yourself is, Why don't Mom and Dad dig my pals? Are your folks clueing in to something you're not, or are they just being overly picky?

Remember, parents have feelings too. They may have trouble facing the fact that their baby is growing up and will soon be leaving the nest. Naturally your folks are bummed to discover that you'd rather hang out at the mall with your buds than stay home and play Scrabble with them. And they may even be a little jealous of your new pals and blame them for stealing you away.

Let your folks know that you're not rejecting them but that you need to start bonding with kids your own age. And try not to blow them off completely. A few hours of family bonding can go a long way.

Another question to ask yourself is, Do my folks really know my friends? Parents, like most people, are terrified of the unknown. Solution: Invite your buds to hang at your house so your folks can get to know them. Once your parents have a clue about who you've been hanging with, they should feel better about your spending time with your new pals.

Also keep in mind that parents (yes, even yours—no, really) are often very wise. There may be a good reason why they don't dig your buds. Have your grades slipped, or have you been getting into trouble since you joined the new crew? If so, you should consider listening to your parents' advice and finding some new pals.

Peer Pressure

Whether it's the pressure to smoke, do drugs, ditch class, blow off your parents, or buy trendy clothes, peer pressure can be bad news. Pressure from your buds can affect everything from how you dress, to who you date, to whether or not you work hard in school. But most people don't realize that peer pressure can also have a good side. The right group of friends can encourage you to do positive things, like working hard in school, pursuing your passions, and being considerate of your pals' feelings. Sometimes sticking with your group amounts to nothing more than making a few small compromises. Sure, you may have to go along with your pals for pizza even though you're dying for a burrito. But last time I checked, minor

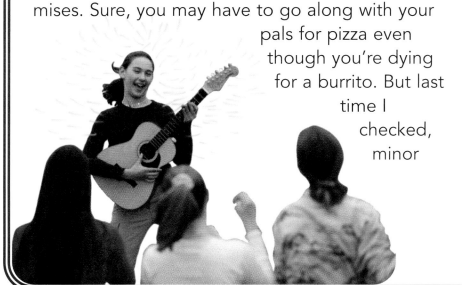

lunch disappointments never hurt anyone. Of course, in a bad situation with the wrong group of pals, peer pressure can get pretty ugly. Comments like these are a sign that your buds are putting negative pressure on you:

"Don't be such a geek."
"Everybody else is doing it!"
"Who's going to find out?"
"Can't you just let go and have a good time?"

Sound familiar? If your answer is yes, then it sounds as if you've already been on the receiving end of negative peer pressure. These examples are exactly the kinds of things that not-so-good friends say to pressure you into doing something against your better judgment. It doesn't matter whether they're trying to convince you to blow off class, wear only expensive clothes, or sample some gin from your parents' liquor cabinet. The point is that they're trying to make you feel as though there's something wrong with you if you don't want to go along with the group. But the truth is that there's nothing wrong with being yourself—especially if that means being smart enough not to get yourself into trouble. Trust me, if your friends are pressuring you to do things you don't want to do, it's your friends who have the problem—not you!

People your age are more susceptible to peer pressure for a couple of reasons. First, in these confusing years, your pals are really important to you. What they think matters, and most of the time, you'd rather go along with the group than risk being rejected. Second, you're probably having some major "Who am I?" moments lately. It's natural to look

to your buds for help figuring out what you like and what's important to you.

As it turns out, some of us gals are more susceptible to negative peer pressure than others. Girls who are insecure tend to crave acceptance from their buds because it makes them feel special. These girls judge their own self-worth by the opinions of their peers. They bend over backward to follow the group because they are terrified of being rejected. Girls who are totally self-confident are less likely to be influenced by peer pressure. They have a strong sense of who they are and what they believe in, and they aren't easily swayed by what other people think.

You're bound to run into peer pressure in the next few years, so you may as well prepare yourself for it. Your best defense is to steer clear of situations in which you're likely to feel pressured. So skip the wild parties if you don't want to drink. And before you even think about giving in to the group, you should ask yourself the following questions:

Does this go against my values?
Will I still respect and feel good about myself if I give in?
Will this affect the goals that I have set for myself?
Do I really want to do this, or am I just following
the crowd?

If something doesn't feel right, don't do it. If your pals can't accept that, it may be time to find a new group of friends.

One last thing: If you think that you can get off the hook for some poor choice of behavior because "my friends made me do it," think again. Peer pressure may be powerful, but it isn't mind control, and it's no excuse for being a fool. The truth is that no matter who influences your decisions, they are still yours to make. If you'd rather let your friends think for you than think for yourself, that's your problem, but you're still responsible for the results. After all, you could have said no.

The Facts About Popularity

6

You get invited to the best parties, and you hang with only the coolest kids in school. Whether this sounds like your wildest dream (or nightmare) or your actual life, you should know that even popularity has its downside.

What Does It Really Mean?

Everybody knows that popular kids are cool, trendy, known and envied by everyone, and kind of snobby about it—right? Well, actually, this common belief is just plain wrong. Being popular means that you're well liked . . . period. Those stuck-up girls may think that they're the greatest, but people outside their little clique may envy them without actually liking them. And that means they're not really popular.

The secret to being well liked is to be, well, likeable. Research shows that popular people have certain qualities—such as being friendly, kind, and cooperative—that draw people to them. And most truly popular people don't have to work at it. It just comes naturally. If you have to spend most of your waking hours scheming about how to become more popular, it may not be worth the effort. You might be better off thinking about how to be happier with yourself or how to be a friendlier, kinder person.

Maybe you don't want to be popular, and that's fine too, as long as you're not avoiding people because of insecurity. For most people, having a few close friends is more important than being liked by everyone. And even the most popular kids are bound to find a few people they just don't click with.

The "In" Crowd

Every school is different, but most have one group of people whom everyone considers to be the "in" crowd. These are the kids everyone knows but not everyone necessarily likes. This crowd can get snotty and may be overly selective about whom they hang out with. Sometimes these kids are just plain rude—at least to people outside of the clique. On the other hand, sometimes those who aren't in the in crowd assume that the people in it must be snobs, without getting to know them first.

If getting into the in crowd is your version of Fantasy

not too cool

kinda cool

Island, there are some things you should know. First, kids in the cool clique don't necessarily have more fun than the rest of us. Most of these kids feel a lot of pressure to keep up appearances. Unlike those who are naturally well liked, kids in the in crowd often have to work hard at being seen as cool. They're always careful to say the right thing and wear the right clothes. Sometimes "cool kids" may feel as though being cool isn't worth the effort.

Beyond the "Out" Crowd

very cool

Not hanging with the cool kids is one thing. For most of us, as long as we have a good set of buds, we're happy campers. But what about those kids whom it seems like no one really likes? Why are they unpopular, and who decided that they were?

What makes someone unpopular? Kids who show off or act spoiled, lazy, dishonest, or inconsiderate are usually not well liked. You probably know a few people who fit that description. If they made an effort to be nicer people and better friends, they would probably find their popularity growing.

Other reasons for unpopularity may be harder to fix. Kids who are overweight, handicapped, unathletic, poor, or unattractive can have a hard time, even though these things are completely out of their control. You may feel relieved not to be in their shoes, and that may lead you to put them down. Making jokes about the overweight girl in your class may seem harmless, and you may not mean to be cruel. But if hurting someone's feelings is your idea of a good time, you definitely need to get a life! There will probably always be someone who thinks it's funny to mock people who aren't popular, but that doesn't make it okay for you to do so.

If you're the one being teased, try to stay tough. I know that it's much easier said than done, because being left out all of the time can feel like a living hell. But trust me, things will get better as you get older. And if you can learn to be happy with yourself as you are, other people will definitely follow your lead. Besides, the kind of people who think it's cool to have a good time at your expense are bound to get what they deserve eventually. In the meantime, they aren't worthy of your energy. Remember, they're the ones with the problem, not you!

Fights and Friction

7

True or false: Real friends always agree, never get on each other's nerves, and never, ever fight. If you answered "true," welcome to the real world! The fact is that even the best of buds fight from time to time. Not only is fighting completely normal, but it can be a good way to let off steam and reestablish the rules of the friendship. That is, of course, as long as you fight fairly.

Fighting fairly means telling the other person exactly how you feel, why you are upset, and what she can do to make it up to you. Fighting fairly means that you resist using your intimate knowledge of your pal to say things that you know will hurt her. The silent treatment, wild rampages, and physical violence are not part of fighting fairly. In a fair fight, each party clearly expresses her feelings and is prepared to compromise.

Friends fight about everything, but some sources of friction are way more common than others. The rest of this chapter focuses on a few common causes of friendship friction and how to deal.

Full-Court Pressure

Friends don't pressure friends to do anything they're uncomfortable with . . . ever! If someone tries to pressure you into doing something that's against your better judgment, take that person off your list of "friends." Friends respect each other's values and beliefs. They like each other for who they are, not who they want the other person to be.

If you're feeling pressured, don't be afraid to say no. Tell your friends that you just don't share their interest in drinking, smoking, shoplifting, or whatever, and leave it at that. A good friend should take no for an answer. If you feel that you have to compromise your values to stay in a friendship, it's probably time to bail out!

Competition and Jealousy

No matter how above-all-that you think you are, the truth is that occasional bouts of jealousy and competitiveness are basic facts of friendship. Sure, you're close, and yes, you respect each other. But there will still be moments when you wish you were the one with the expensive outfit or the supercute boyfriend. And though you may be rooting for your bud to get the slot next to yours on the basketball team, frankly, if it's between the two of ya, you'll be looking out for number one!

Brief pangs of jealousy and competition are totally normal. What's not cool is when your friend is so jealous or competitive that she cuts you down, sabotages your efforts, or tries to make you feel bad about yourself. To nip her jealousy in the bud, try pumping up her ego. Help her see how much she has going for her by stressing her strong points. And try to encourage her to develop her own special talents so she won't feel as blown away by yours. Ditto for the competitive pal. Chances are her fierce behavior just means that she's feelin' insecure. Rather than catching her competitive spirit, try backing off and giving her a few words of encouragement instead.

If you're the one with the jealous or competitive streak, you may need to focus more on your own strengths rather than hers. Your pal may have a ton going for her, but I'm willing to bet that you're pretty special too.

Guys in the Middle

Are you and your pal crushing over the same dude? Or has she been blowing you off in favor of her beau? Maybe you're not so wild about her latest date. Or maybe she's the one who's been dissing your latest fling. Whatever the problem, I'm not surprised. The fact is that fights over guys top the list of the most common sources of friendship friction.

Is your bud's new guy stealing all of her attention? We all know the story: They're tucked away in their little love nest, and you're all alone, pining over the time you used to spend with her. It may help to tell your friend how you feel and ask her to make a little room for you. This might also be a good time to seek out new friends to help fill the void until your girlfriend comes back to earth—and she will come back.

Things can get even more complicated when you and your bud dig the same dude. All that nasty jealousy and competition stuff comes to play in full force. But before you desert your pal for a guy, be sure to think long and hard about whether he's really worth busting up your friendship. Chances are the answer will be "No way!" At your age, friendships tend to last a whole lot longer (and are a lot more satisfying) than those steamy romances.

One last thing: Don't even think of going after your best bud's ex. I know he's a hottie, but it just won't work. No matter who ended the relationship, she's bound to feel hurt and jealous if you make a move before the smoke has cleared (and I mean *really* cleared). Find someone else to crush on, and make a pact with your pals to do the same when it comes to your leftovers.

Double-Faced Friends

Does your pal act all lovey-dovey, palsey-walsey when you're around and then plunge the knife in as soon as you turn your back? Bad-mouthing a friend is never cool. In fact, when it comes to friendships, behind-the-back dissings are clear grounds for dismissal. But remember that you can't always trust what you hear via the grapevine. Before you cut her out of all your pictures, confront your pal and ask her if what you've heard is true. Give her a chance to defend herself. And remember that there is a fine line between venting and dissing. If you're upset with a friend, tell her directly rather than complaining behind her back.

Dear Vicky,
My friend June told me that our mutual friend Samantha told her that our other friend Carmen is really mad at me about something I said to her. Now the whole crew is mad at me, and I still have no idea what I did wrong! What should I do?
—Dissed and Confused

Dear Dissed,
Sounds as though you and your buds have some major communication problems! If Carmen is upset with you, she should tell you directly. Now that the damage is done, your best bet is to talk to her. Tell her that you're sorry if you did something to hurt her, and that you wish she had

come to you. If she refuses to talk, be sure to point out to your friends how unfair they're all being by accusing you and not even giving you the chance to defend yourself.

As our pal "Dissed" discovered, when it comes to friendships, communication is key! When friends fight, sometimes all you need to work things out is a good heart-to-heart chat. Other times you may decide that it's necessary to move on.

Damage Control

Okay, you've been dogged, and you're mega-steamed. But before you throw in the towel, you may want to try a little repair work. The first thing to do is talk it out. The silent treatment may get your basic point ("I'm steamed") across, but it won't solve the problem. And pretending that everything's cool when it's not can only make things worse. After all, you'll be fuming, and she'll be thinking that it's business-as-usual.

If you're fuming, approach your pal and tell her exactly what's bugging you. Be as clear and specific as you can. Assume that she doesn't have a clue about what she did wrong, and spell it out for her. And don't be afraid to tell her about the hurt you are feeling. If she doesn't take your feelings seriously, she probably wasn't much of a friend to begin with.

The hardest part of settling a disagreement is saying you're sorry. But though apologizing may not always be fun, it's a friendship necessity. Don't assume that you and your pal have an apology understanding unless the words "I'm sorry" have been uttered. A formal apology is essential to setting things straight. Remember to be clear about how you feel and why you are sorry. (e.g., "I'm sorry I shared your secrets with the whole world; it was the wrong thing to do.") You want your pal to know that you realize what you did to upset her.

You and your pal should end your little chat by talking about where things went wrong. Then you can work out a strategy for nipping future problems in the bud. For example, if your friend blabbed your secrets, make sure that both of you are clear on the fact that from here on in, all secrets should stay secret.

Tips for Blowing Off Steam

Having a casual chat with a pal who's dissed you is easier said than done. How can you be cool as a cuke when you're ready to blow? Since screaming in her face will probably make matters worse, it's best to calm yourself down before you make your move. The following are proven methods for blowing off steam:

Write your pal a letter. Feel free to express yourself, even if that means calling her every name in the book. Just be sure to destroy the evidence when you're finished—and don't even think about sending it!

Scream into your pillow and give it a few punches for good measure. It's safer than going ballistic on your pal and kinder than taking it out on your kid brother or your cat.

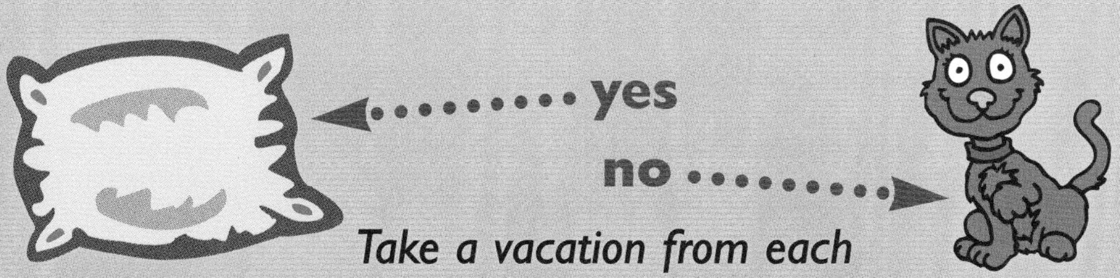

yes

no

Take a vacation from each other. Tell your pal that you're upset but that you're not ready to deal. A few days apart will help you both collect your thoughts and calm down.

> *Get some outside advice. Discuss the situation with your mom, your big sis, your boyfriend, or anyone you trust who isn't already involved. But resist the urge to vent to mutual friends.*

Is It Over?

Sometimes your best efforts aren't enough to save a dying friendship. The fact is that even the best of friends can grow apart. Here are some clues that your friendship is ready to sizzle and burn:

> *The girl really gets on your last nerve, and you just don't enjoy being with her like you used to.*
>
> *You feel angry or sad most of the time when you're with her.*
>
> *She's started experimenting with things (for example, drinking, smoking, sex) that you're not comfortable with, and she's pressuring you to do the same.*
>
> *She keeps flaking on plans with you and doesn't return your phone calls.*
>
> *She has done something that is absolutely unforgivable. Worse, even after you've tried to talk it through, she refuses to apologize or even admit that she did anything wrong.*
>
> *The friendship is just not that important to you anymore.*

Ending It

As someone somewhere must have said sometime, "Saying good-bye is hard to do." Even if your soon-to-be-ex-friend totally bulldozed you, you still may feel sad about cutting her loose. And sometimes you're the one who gets left out in the cold. If your former best friend has decided to move on to bigger and better things, you may be feeling pretty low.

Good exit strategies:

Stay civil. Don't be rude or ignore her completely. If you pass her in the hall, just say "hi" and leave it at that.

Try to resist bad-mouthing the girl. It will only make you look weak.

Try not to take it too personally. Sometimes friendships end. It's a fact of life. Not every friendship is worth saving, and not everyone has to be your friend forever. When a friendship ends, it doesn't mean that there's something wrong with you, only that there was something wrong with the friendship.

What if your ex-pal's not playing by the rules? You know the type: She corners all of your mutual buds so that she can rant and rave about what a creep you are. If she's dissing you, it's definitely okay to defend yourself. Calmly explain your side to your friends, or better yet, point out to your pals how uncool she is to be airing your dirty laundry to everyone in sight. And then leave it at that—don't sink down to her level and start slinging the mud back at her. Then you'll both come out looking like losers.

Losing a friend can be tough, even if it was totally meant to be. You may miss some of the things you used to do together, or you just may miss having someone to spend time with. Give yourself a chance to grieve over the loss. Then move on. There are plenty of new friends waiting for you to find them.

What's the Word?

clique   An exclusive group or circle of friends.

competitive   Measuring yourself against other people and wanting to be better at something than they are.

conformity   Acting or appearing the same way as the largest or most powerful group of people.

peer pressure   Pressure to behave a certain way or to do certain things from people your age or in your social group.

rejection   Being turned down or told no—for example, when asking someone to join you in an activity.

self-confidence   Belief in yourself, your abilities, and your positive qualities.

self-worth   Belief in and respect for yourself and your value as a person; self-esteem.

supportive   Being helpful, understanding, and considerate; encouraging and accepting someone's actions or behavior.

It's a Girl's World:
helpful info

Web sites

Cyberteens Zine: http://www.cyberteens.com/ezine

Girls, Inc.: http://www.girlsinc.com

Girls On: http://www.girlson.com

Girlspace's Love It/Loathe It:
http://www.kotex.com/girlspace.com/loveloathe

gURL Online Magazine: http://www.gURL.com

SmartGirl Internette: http://www.smartgirl.com

TeenSpeak: http://www.teenspeak.com

Magazines

Blue Jean Magazine
P.O. Box 507
Victor, NY 14564-0507
(888) 4-BLU-JEAN [425-5326]

Girls' Life
4517 Harford Road
Baltimore, MD 21214
Web site: http://www.girlslife.com

New Moon: The Magazine for Girls and Their Dreams
P.O. Box 3620
Duluth, MN 55803
(800) 381-4743
Web site: http://www.newmoon.org

By the Book: *further reading*

Anderson, Peggy King. *First Day Blues*. Seattle, WA: Parenting Press, 1993.

Baker, Camy. *Love You Like a Sister*. New York: Bantam Doubleday Dell Books for Young Readers, 1998.

Bode, Janet. *Trust and Betrayal: Real Life Stories of Friends and Enemies*. New York: Bantam Doubleday Dell Books for Young Readers, 1997.

Braithwaite, Althea. *Being Friends*. Milwaukee, WI: Gareth Stevens, 1998.

Feller, Robyn M. *Everything You Need to Know About Peer Pressure*. Rev. ed. New York: Rosen Publishing Group, 1997.

Livingston, Myra Cohn, ed. *A Time to Talk: Poems of Friendship*. New York: Margaret McElderberry Books, 1992.

Michelle, Lonnie. *How Kids Make Friends: Secrets for Making Lots of Friends, No Matter How Shy You Are*. Evanston, IL: Freedom Publishing Co., 1997.

Romain, Trevor. *Cliques, Phonies, and Other Baloney*. Minneapolis, MN: Free Spirit Publishing, 1998.

Rosenberg, Ellen. *Growing Up Feeling Good*. New York: Puffin Books, 1995.

Schneider, Meg F. *Popularity Has Its Ups and Downs*.

Parsippany, NJ: Julian Messner Books, 1992.

Seamans, Sally. *The Care and Keeping of Friends.*
    Middleton, WI: Pleasant Company, 1996.

Weston, Carol. *For Girls Only: Wise Words, Good
    Advice.* New York: Avon Books, 1998.

———. *Girltalk: All the Stuff Your Sister Never Told You.*
    New York: HarperPerennial, 1997.

Index

Credits

About the Author

Victoria Shaw received her Ph.D. in psychology from Princeton University. She has taught classes in child development at Teachers College of Columbia University and conducted research concerning adolescents. She has also participated in Big Brothers/Big Sisters and served as a social work intern in Connecticut. Ms. Shaw and her family live in New York City.

Photo Credits

All photos by Thaddeus Hardin.

Series Design

Laura Murawski

Layout

Oliver Rosenberg

DATE DUE
